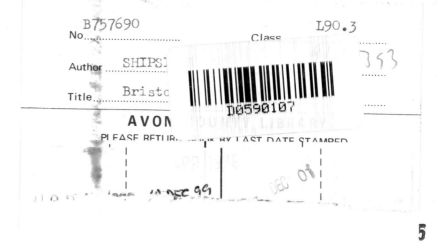

Bristol: profile of a city

BRISTOL:
profile of a city

Shipsides and Eason

THE REDCLIFFE PRESS

First published in November 1979 by
Redcliffe Press Ltd. Bristol

Second impression January 1980

ISBN 0 905459 21 0

Printed in Great Britain by
Burleigh Ltd., Bristol

Contents

Illustrations

The Avon Gorge Hotel

The Spas of Bristol

WHATEVER BRISTOL means to most people today, in the eighteenth century its fame was largely due to its Spas, and to one in particular. One of the extraordinary features of the Hotwell Spa was its rapid rise to fame and one of the saddest, its equally swift decline. At its height it was a fashionable resort with important visitors, the inspiration for poets, painters and novelists. Yet, by the end of the century it was a doomed and decaying district of dilapidated lodging houses.

It all began with a hot spring which gushed out of an opening at the foot of St. Vincent's Rock almost underneath the present Suspension Bridge. At high tide the spring was some twenty-six feet below river level, but when the tide ebbed, it poured out at sixty gallons a minute. The water was not exactly hot—rather tepid in fact at seventy-six degrees—but it brought fame and the fashionable to this spot, a mile from the city centre.

The first record of the spring was made by the topographer William Wyrcestre in the fifteenth century, when he noted, 'a fountain on the side of Ghyston Cliff, towards the bottom of the river, and it is as warm as milk or like the water of Bath'. By 1650 it had become more generally known and drew recommendations from doctors like Dr. Venner, who pre-

9

scribed it for those 'who have hot livers, feeble brains and red pimply faces'. Royal patronage came with the visit of Catherine of Braganza, the wife of Charles II, in 1677 and the possibilities of the place as a health spa were realised. The Society of Merchant Venturers, as Lords of the Manor of Clifton, leased the well to a group of local businessmen who built the Hotwell House on the small rocky ledge overlooking the river.

All the sick and ailing who came expected miracles from the spa water, and why not when Sketchley's Bristol Directory for 1775 could advertise that 'the diseases in which Bristol waters are properly prescribed are, internal haemorrhages, blood spittings, dysentery and immoderate flux, purulent ulcers of the viscera; hence in consumptions, the dropsy, scurvy with heat, stone gravel, stranguary, the habitable gout, scorbatic rheumatism, diabetes, slow fever, atrophy, venereal disease, cancer, gleets of both sexes, king's evil etc. . . .'? The bottling of the water was a considerable industry and Defoe on his visit in 1724, noted fifteen glass-houses 'which are more than in London, for sending the Hotwell water not only over England but all over the world'. This water was really popular and didn't seem to suffer a setback even on November 1st, 1774, when it ran red like blood, apparently affected by the earthquake in Lisbon.

The Hotwell season began in April and lasted until September, nicely fitting in with the Bath season which ran from September to May. Finally, two kinds of visitor came to the Hotwell; the really ill who took the cure and the elegant who took the waters as part of a fashionable round of pleasure. Their daily routine began with a ride to the Pump Room to drink the medicinal water, then a relaxing game of cards before listening to the concert provided by a small orchestra. The afternoon was equally arduous; perhaps a walk along the tree-lined Dowry Parade, or, if wet, a stroll along the colonnade of shops erected in 1789. Remains of the small colonnade survive as houses. In the evening, a return visit would be made to the Pump Room for a Ball or other entertainment.

These delights were obviously intended for the hale and hearty, but one Hotwell physician regretted 'that the female invalids, who are for the most part at that period of life when public entertainments have their peculiar relish, err in no one instance so much as in the indulgence of dancing, an exercise most salutary to lungs that are sound, but as injurious to those that are unsound'. Sadly, it was those with unsound lungs, often dying of tuberculosis, who had their last flings at the Hotwell and the increasing number of deaths was a contributory cause of the Spa's decline also. It still had a few years to run and imitated Bath in appointing a Master of Ceremonies whose task it was to preserve decorum in the public festivities. He drew up a list of rules of etiquette, including one 'that no gentleman shall appear with a sword or spurs in these Rooms, or on a Ball night, in boots'.

Francis Greenway's Assembly Rooms

The Spa's success lay in providing entertainment cheaply and accommodating visitors reasonably in nearby lodging houses. From 1727 onwards, new houses were built providing a residential centre for the Spa. Dowry Square had been started in 1717 and many surgeons set up their profitable practices there. At No. 6, Dr. Thomas Beddoes ran his Pneumatic Institute, where he aimed to treat tuberculosis by inhalation. He was convinced that air, modified in some way, was essential for the successful treatment of the disease. When he learned that 'a lady had her distressing symptoms all removed from living the winter in a room with four cows', he thought that he had found the answer. Hotwells landladies, however, complained that they 'had not furnished their rooms for cattle'. Beddoes continued at the Institute but the house has a more permanent claim to fame, for here the young physician, Humphry Davy, first experimented with nitrous oxide before he went on to invent the miners' safety lamp.

The spiritual requirements of the visitors were also catered for, and considering the high mortality rate that was just as well. Lady Hope and her friend, Lady Glenorchy, came as patients, and in 1788 opened Hope Chapel for Congregationalists. This chapel was due for demolition, but has been saved by its new use as a centre for community activities. Holy Trinity, the parish church of Hotwells, is a beautiful example of C. R. Cockerell's Greek Revival style. Its interior was gutted during the 'blitz', but the whole church has been successfully restored.

The Colonnade

The end of the century was to see the end of the Hotwell Spa. The end really began in 1788, when a new tenant had to pay an increased rent for the lease of the Hotwell House and Pump, and he in turn had to charge more for the pleasures he offered. The fashionable visitors gradually decreased while the invalids died in increasing numbers. In 1800 also, the

Dowry Square, Hotwells

St. Mary Redcliffe

Sion Hill

water supply gave serious trouble; the pollution and stench from the Avon offended the nose of the more genteel guests. By 1822, the old Hotwell House had been taken down, the lodging-house keepers were bankrupt and the silence of the grave replaced the once lively dance music. Only a portion of the colonnade remains to bear witness to the glory that this area once knew, though the lovely old houses of Dowry Square are being restored and lived in as they should be.

The Hotwell may have declined, but the future belonged to Clifton-on-the-Hill. Sion Spring had been discovered in 1793, when a local attorney living on Sion Hill made a boring through the limestone rock and reached a spring of water yielding 74,000 gallons daily and having a temperature nearly as high as the Hotwell. He built a small Pump room and Baths and set up in competition with the Hotwell below. Once it was realised that the heights of Clifton were delightful in themselves, building began in earnest. The once isolated houses of the rich were to be closed in by great terraces, rising above one another on the cliffs overhanging the river. The rush of speculative buildings was temporarily halted by the French Revolutionary Wars, but the character of the new Clifton had been determined, and the Mall, Prince's Buildings, Royal York Crescent were the first of many fine terraces.

The Clifton visitors soon felt the need for an Assembly Room to be the centre of the social scene. In 1806, Felix Farley reported that 'a meeting of the nobility and gentry of Clifton took place at Sion Hill Pump for the purpose of considering a proposal for building a new Assembly Room with card tables etc. Two plans were submitted, one for erection on Sion Hill, the other on the Mall.' The Mall site was chosen and the new Assembly Rooms were designed by Francis Greenway to be 'a spacious and elegant hotel and Assembly Rooms with a noble reception saloon and tea-room, a ballroom highly furnished and decorated, and a handsome cardroom'. The Hotel would include 'a shop for pastry and confectionery with an adjoining room for soups, fruits and ices'. For a while the Hotel and Rooms flourished. In 1830, the future Queen Victoria was taken on a Royal Progress by her mother, the Duchess of Kent, and it was from the balcony of this hotel that the ten-year-old princess waved for the first time to her Bristol public. Today, the Clifton Antiques Market occupies part of the Assembly Rooms.

The Sion Hill Spa was short-lived, but an attempt was made to revive it at the end of the nineteenth century. George Newnes, the magazine proprietor, was given permission to construct a hydraulic cliff-railway from Hotwells to Sion Hill, on condition that he restored the old Spa by building a Pump Room at the end of Prince's Buildings. The enterprise was doomed to failure and the building finally became an ordinary hotel, the Grand Spa Hotel. The ornate Pump Room, which once housed spring water and mineral baths, is now buried deep in the recesses of the re-named Avon Gorge Hotel.

St. James' Priory Church, Haymarket

Bristol Churches

BRISTOL IS a city of really beautiful churches, some old, some new; some thriving, some threatened with closure; but so long as its fabric stands then a church remains part of the life of the city.

St. James' Priory Church overlooks the Haymarket, one of the busiest thoroughfares in the city, on the edge of the Broadmead shopping centre. Although it seems so much a part of the modern city, it stood originally outside the walls as part of St. James' Priory, which flourished for three hundred and twenty years as a cell of the Benedictine Tewkesbury Abbey. Robert, Earl of Gloucestershire, a natural son of Henry II, began it in 1129 at the same time as he built the Great Keep of the castle. Tradition has it that he set aside every tenth stone brought from Caen for the Chapel. The Priory was really a whole community outside the city; farms, cloisters, dormitories and outbuildings were necessary to support

17

the religious foundation. Its size ensured that it shared the fate of all such establishments at the Dissolution of the Monasteries in 1543 and its lands were bought up by Robert Brayne, a London merchant tailor turned property developer. The cloisters were allowed to fall into picturesque ruins, the outbuildings were built over and only the Chapel survived. But what a survival! Just look at the west front and see the Norman arcade of interlaced arches, three of which are pierced for circular-headed windows, and then marvel at the exquisite small wheel-window, one of the earliest of its kind in England. This front is a lasting tribute to the skill of the Norman architects and its solidity and strength ensured its survival. Robert Brayne demolished all the Priory buildings but he was persuaded by the parishioners to sell them the Nave for their new parish church. They could well afford to buy it, for the parish of St. James' was a populous and prosperous one and many important men were worshippers at the church. The registers date from 1559 and are a social history in themselves, carefully listing the effects of such disasters as the Plague and the Great Floods. The names of prominent men appear, including those of John and Charles Wesley who lived in the parish. John is listed as 'a preacher in the Horsefair', and his brother's children were baptised here, five alas buried as infants in the churchyard. When Elizabeth I stopped on her visit to the city in 1594, the register reveals that she was presented with 'a handsome prayer-book costing 6d'.

The interior of the church still has its massive Norman pillars and some very handsome monuments, including one to Sir James Russell, Governor of Nevis in the West Indies, who died in 1674. High up in the roof are corbels with carved, painted heads in the style of the fifteenth century. St. James' Fair, held annually in the open space before the church, was one of the most celebrated in England. The Fair originated from a feast day during the week of Pentecost, when relics were venerated and indulgences earned by those who brought alms. The feast inevitably developed into a trading fair, which degenerated so much that in 1837 it was ended.

St. Mary Redcliffe is without doubt Bristol's most beautiful church and one can be forgiven for thinking that it is the cathedral; it is really just a parish church, though the most painted, photographed and celebrated in verse and song. Elizabeth I's praise of it is well quoted but she also made a

St. Stephen's Church

-FRANK SHIPSIDES - 1978 -

St. Mark's, the Lord Mayor's Chapel

more practical appreciation of it when she gave the church lands which had been confiscated by her brother, Edward VI, ordering that 'the rents, issues, and profits thereof should be employed in maintaining and keeping the said church in its wonted beauty and repair, it being the greatest ornament to these parts of the kingdom'.

Its position on the red cliffs at the water's edge above the docks and at the very centre of ship-building and industry, is the key to its history. Since 1180, merchants had begun and ended their journeys and voyages at the shrine of Our Lady of Red Cliff, and to them, and especially William Canynges, five times Mayor of the city, we owe the church as it is now. This wealthy ship-owner built himself a mansion within sight and sound of the source of his wealth, overlooking the harbour from which his ships traded, and he spent a great part of his fortune rebuilding his parish church. The hexagonal north porch has the most elaborate carving in stonework, for at one time its inner porch housed a relic of the Blessed Virgin, past which seafarers filed in thanksgiving after a voyage. The relic has gone but there are many more treasures inside the church itself. John Cabot was a Redcliffe man and sailed from its harbour to Newfoundland, bringing back the rib of a great whale which now hangs in the Nave. There is a unique wooden, painted effigy of Elizabeth I, probably painted on her first visit and intended to be used as a ship's figurehead. William Canynges deserved two tombs and he got them; one shows him as the fifteenth century merchant he was, and the other as the priest which he became after the death of his wife. Sir William Penn, Admiral and General, famous father of an even more famous son, lies beneath a large, black stone in the south transept. He was a true son of Bristol, and he combined the careers of seaman, merchant and soldier, culminating in his most celebrated exploit, the capture of Jamaica for England without the loss of a single man. He had generously lent Charles I a great deal of money, so when Charles II found it difficult to repay his father's debts, Penn's son William asked for a grant of land in Virginia instead, and thus in 1661 founded Pennsylvania.

On the north side of College Green facing the Cathedral, is the Chapel of St. Mark's, known familiarly as the Lord Mayor's Chapel. Like the Church of St. James' it is the only surviving part of an earlier foundation and in some ways its story is similar. It was part of the medieval Hospital of the Gaunts built in 1230 by Maurice de Gaunt, where one hundred poor people were to be fed daily. It soon became a religious community with a Master, chaplains and twelve poor scholars as choristers. The foundation was never wealthy but this did not stop its dissolution in 1549. This time however, the property was not bought by a professional grabber of church lands, but by the Corporation of Bristol for £1,000. The buildings were adapted for various uses but the Chapel was kept, making Bristol the only city in England to own a chapel for its own use as an official place of worship.

Much of St. Mark's is hidden from view by the surrounding buildings, but the Front on College Green is well known. The chapel is interesting as giving an idea of what the smaller religious houses were like, for few survive. The Poyntz chapel is the most delightful chantry in the city, erected by Sir Robert Poyntz of Iron Acton, a friend of both Henry VII and Henry VIII. His chantry has everything; a fan-traceried roof, a floor inlaid with sixteenth century Spanish tiles and beautiful Flemish stained glass windows. St. Mark's is the best place to see a collection of monuments depicting costume from the thirteenth to the nineteenth centuries. It begins with the founder, Maurice de Gaunt, in his chain mail and his descendant Sir Maurice Berkeley in full armour. Then comes a bishop in Tudor vestments; an Elizabethan merchant, and the rare monument to a Jacobean schoolboy, John Cookin, with pen, inkhorn and book behind him.

St. Mark's is the civic church, but St. Stephen's is loved as the city's parish church. It was built in the thirteenth century to serve a new parish outside the city wall, but since the external rebuilding in the fifteenth century, it has been taken into the heart of the city and into the hearts of its citizens. When, after the War, other parishes were amalgamated with it, it became 'St. Stephen's with St. Nicholas with St. Leonard', strengthening its claim to be the city's parish church. The tall perpendicular tower and the great west window were built by a first citizen, John Shipward, whose house adjoined the church. Apart from beautifying his parish church, he was notable for his involvement in the Battle of Nibley Green fought in 1470, the last 'private' battle recorded in England. The church is truly an archive of Bristol's history. The city's part in Atlantic exploration is recalled by a wall monument to Martin Pring, navigator

St. James' West Front

and explorer, who sailed with fifty men and two ships to land in Cape Cod, New England in 1603.

Two important civic societies take an interest in St. Stephen's; the Society of Merchant Venturers and the Antient Society of St. Stephen's Ringers. When the great west window suffered war damage in 1940, it was repaired and reglazed at their joint cost and the Coats of Arms of both societies are incorporated in the new glazing. The original Society of Bellringers was probably a pre-Reformation Guild dedicated to the craft of bell-ringing, but soon it took on a social and benevolent role in the parish. As customs changed, the ringing of bells became less important and the society took in new members, sometimes from outside the parish but always of superior social status. This led to some degeneration but curiously enough, the conviviality and festivity kept the society alive. It was at the annual dinner in 1873 that the Rector rebuked the diners for their lack of benevolence and shamed them into dedicating themselves once more to the preservation of the church and its precincts, a role which the society has pursued ever since.

Now, what was this annual bacchanalian festivity which brought disgrace to the society? On November 17th, the members met to celebrate the accession day of Elizabeth I, their patroness, with songs and general merriment. Today, it is no longer an occasion for excesses but a retention of many interesting customs such as hand-bell ringing, singing of old songs such as 'The Golden Days of Good Queen Bess' with each guest singing a verse, and then the procession of the Don. This procession is of obscure origin, but in essence it involves past Masters parading in solemn order, preceded by a bell-man carrying an antique bust of Queen Bess and a stuffed fox. The need to celebrate England's victory over the Armada of the Spanish Don is understandable; the fox was added in the unecumenical days of Protestant mistrust of Catholicism. It is said that Charles II's child-less Queen Catherine, a Catholic, suffered a miscarriage when his pet fox jumped on her bed. The frightened Queen lost the last hope of a Stuart heir to the throne who, though legitimate, might have shared her Catholic leanings. The Annual Dinner is preceded by the Annual Service when the Ringers process to St. Stephen's in great style.

Bristol has the finest parish church and the only Civic church in England, but there are other denominations which are uniquely served in the city. In Broadmead, tucked away almost unnoticed in a busy street, is the oldest building for Methodist worship in the world, known just as the New Room. John Wesley did not build it originally to be a separate church but rather as a place where he could hold services when denied the use of Anglican pulpits. It was only after his death that the New Room in the Horsefair became a Chapel for independent Methodists.

The building has many interesting features. It is a galleried chapel with a two-decker pulpit; the service was read from the lower one so that Wesley could deliver his 'plain speaking to plain men' from the upper. The 'parliament clock' on the gallery front could be used to time the sermons which could last up to three hours when John Wesley was in full voice. The atmosphere and spirit of early Methodism is everywhere here, especially in the rooms above the Chapel. John Wesley's bedroom is just as it was when he slept there, so is the room used by his brother Charles, before his marriage; pictures, prints, books and mementoes of all kinds make a visit to this little museum well worth while. It was in the Conference Room that John first commissioned his lay preachers to go forth and spread the 'spiritual holiness' of early Methodism. In 1771 Francis

Two-tier pulpit in the New Room, Horsefair

25

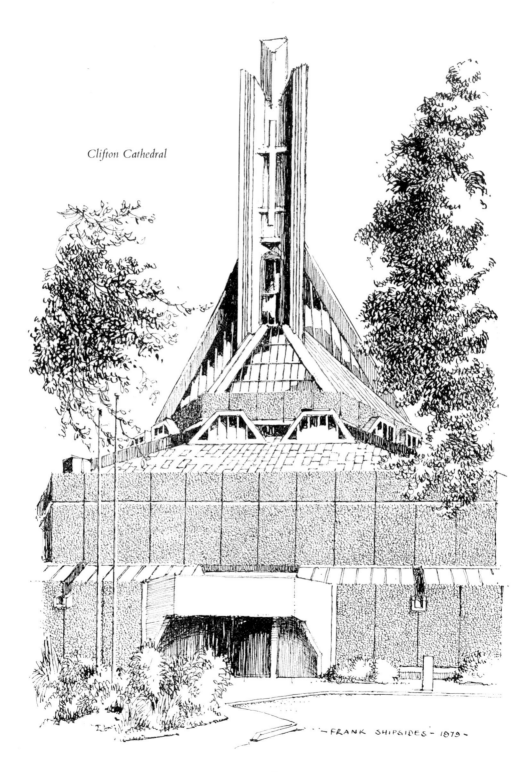

Clifton Cathedral

-FRANK SHIPSIDES- 1879-

26

Asbury answered the call to go to America and set up the first Methodist church in New York. The New Room is therefore high on the list for American tourists anxious to see the birthplace of their Episcopalian church. The stable where preachers could 'bed and bait' their horses is at the side of the Room and two fine life-like statues of the Wesley brothers, holding out their hands in welcome, dominate the two entrances.

Not all churches have their roots firmly fixed in the past, one in particular has its roof daringly flying off into the future. The Church of Saints Peter and Paul is one of the most modern Roman Catholic cathedrals in the world, designed to take account of the Second Vatican Council's liturgical changes. One must abandon all preformed notions of what a cathedral should be like when one enters this award-winning, pre-stressed concrete edifice. It was not of course designed to be an architectural monument but a living church, a parish church for Clifton as well as a new cathedral to replace the old 'Pro'. The main feature of its construction is its hexagonal shape to ensure that all the congregation could see the Mass wherever they were sitting. With the High Altar, hewn from Portland stone, standing functionally in the middle there is a tremendous feeling of space and light and air, so different from the claustrophobic atmosphere of many old cathedrals. A stainless steel tabernacle, a bronze statue of the Virgin, flat carved concrete Stations of the Cross, are all simple in design and in keeping with the spirit of the place.

The Naval Volunteer and the Admiral Benbow

28

The Full Moon, Stokes' Croft

Inns Ancient and Modern

OF THE city's four hundred inns and pubs, the oldest is probably the Hatchet in Frogmore Street. The original house was part of a farm in what was then Frog Lane, the main route out of Bristol to the village of Clifton, before Park Street was opened up. By the end of the sixteenth century, the farmhouse was altered and adapted for its use as an inn; the date 1606 over the door refers to the date in which the inn was first licensed. Frog Lane would have been a very busy highway, with country vehicles and waggons passing along in front of the inn, which at one time was surrounded by an extensive stableyard, with a well to provide water for man and beast.

The area around the Hatchet was radically changed in the 1960s when it was decided to site a new Entertainment Centre in the street and create a new road line. The inn miraculously escaped demolition by being preserved on a traffic island and—altered and enlarged by architects Sir Percy Thomas and Sons—it earned a Civic Trust Award. It was during the alterations that the picturesque façade came to light, after years of hiding behind a skin of lath and plaster. Now, with its early timber frame re-created, the Hatchet is once more a popular inn, though it has lost its extensive stableyard, large gardens and cock-pit. Until 1836, the Dean and Chapter of Bristol Cathedral owned the land on which the Hatchet stands, and it is tempting to think that the sporting Dean Creswicke might have enjoyed the fights here before he was promoted to Wells where he ordered a cock-pit to be constructed outside his dining room window.

The sporting connections of the Hatchet have always been emphasised and many noted pugilists have patronised the inn. Tom Cribb, born in Hanham in 1781, Jem Mace and Tom Sayers, were all Bristol men who used the gardens around the inn as their training grounds. They had to go to London however to find fame and fortune. The Tudor timber front looks especially attractive at night when the lights pick out the heavy, original entrance door and the inn's other glory which cannot be seen easily by day. This is a fine seventeenth-century plaster-work ceiling which extends the whole length of the first floor. This original work of Italian craftsmen also came to light during the restoration and is a real gem.

Why the unique name, the Hatchet? It must refer to the craft of wood-carving, and as Clifton Wood at one time crept down the hillside behind the inn, many woodcutters must have quenched their thirsts in its parlours.

Although the Hatchet occupies the oldest building, it is the Rummer in All Saints Lane which holds Bristol's No. 1 licence. The present inn has been known as the Rummer for over two hundred years, but its history goes back much further than that, for it is built on a portion of the site occupied by an inn since 1250. Many old inns have had changes of name, but the Rummer must surely hold the record. In 1250, it was called the Greene Lattis, keeping this name until 1440 when the premises were enlarged and Thomas Abyndon, a church-warden of All Saints, became its innkeeper. The Abyndon in its turn was incorporated into the nearby Jonas and the building was called simply, the 'New Inn'. Old habits die hard and deeds still referred to it as 'the New Inn, alias Abyndon alias Greene Lattis'. Parts of this earlier hostelry remain in the cellars of the present Rummer which was built in 1743 when a new Exchange was planned for the Bristol merchants. The site in Corn Street was chosen and it became necessary to open up a new thoroughfare to the Market which was to be built behind it. John Wood, the Elder, was the designer of the Exchange and he contrived a new approach to the Rummer as an integral

Ashton Court Mansion

Small Street, Bristol

part of the Exchange and the Market. He set back and largely rebuilt the inn, giving it an entrance into All Saints Lane, as well as retaining the original one in High Street. It was to the High Street entrance that the coaching trade came. John Palmer of Bath had signed a contract with the Postmaster General for the carriage of mail by coach and on August 8th, 1784 the very first coach from London arrived at the Rummer at eleven o'clock at night, after a record-breaking fifteen hour journey. The Rummer was in business as Bristol's first coaching inn and continued until October 21st, 1843 when the last coach left for London, made obsolete by the new Great Western Railway. Incidentally, it is interesting to recall the part played by two Bristol men in this social change. It was John Loudon Macadam, a Bristol engineer, whose invention for improving roads by a process known as macadamisation made possible the golden age of coaching inns, while it was another engineer with strong Bristol connections, Brunel, whose G.W.R. brought that era to an end.

Although the Rummer has been altered internally, there are still some good things within its walls. John Wood installed the lovely newelled staircase when he rebuilt the inn and near the stairs are two other items of note. On a plinth in a prominent position is a magnificent Rummer of beaten copper and wood, which might have served as an inn sign at some stage in its history. A rummer was a large drinking vessel and the sign of a Rummer would have indicated a good drinking house. The imposing clock at the foot of the staircase is typical of the sort which came to be known as Parliament Clocks, when in 1797 a tax of five shillings was put on private clocks and watches. Inns decided to install their own large clocks as a public service and this one at the Rummer is a prime specimen. In 1962, the Berni Brothers bought the Rummer and inaugurated their own brand of social revolution when they set up their first steak bar in the west.

The eighteenth-century historian Seyer indicated on his map of Bristol as it was in 1350 'the Full Moon, an ancient hostellerie', and the present inn is on the second oldest site in the city. It enjoyed an important position, adjacent to the old city boundary with Gloucestershire and originally stood on an isolated and extensive site surrounded by fields. Today, it still seems to stand apart from the hustle of the city, though the Avon House complex does its best to overshadow it.

The Lochiel floating pub

-FRANK SHIPSIDES-1979-

34

The oldest part of the Full Moon is the series of seventeenth-century dormer windows overlooking the narrow Moon Street, but the more familiar outline of the building is from the eighteenth. The magnificent wrought-iron archway at the drive-in from Stokes' Croft indicates its importance as a coaching inn, where the weary traveller would find a splendid place in which to rest, dine and be pleasantly entertained. The huge, airy cellars were filled with wines and spirits, and many a three-bottle man must have been glad to find the 'drunkards' staircase so accommodating. This main staircase leading out of the dining room is the Full Moon's most splendid relic from the seventeenth century. It has twisted columns and remarkably wide, shallow steps which made for easy going when a man was less than steady on his feet.

The White Hart cannot claim to be Bristol's oldest inn but it is associated with Bristol's oldest church, St. James' in the Horsefair. The church was originally part of a Priory erected by Robert, Earl of Gloucester in A.D. 1130. The Priory cloisters and dormitories have gone and all that is left of that foundation is the church itself, with its tower and superb west front rising up behind the White Hart. 1672 is the date prominently displayed on the front and the old doorways lead into an inn which retains all the atmosphere of its heritage. The Bristol Royal Infirmary is just up the road, as it has been since its foundation in 1735. Early physicians and surgeons at the hospital met regularly in the White Hart to sing glees at their Catch Club and today's medical and dental students still congregate here, though they're a little short on glees.

King Street is a veritable museum street with a wealth of architectural subjects of varying dates and styles spanning three hundred years. Prosperous merchants were glad to escape from the old walled city and create a new area of spacious houses in King Street. These elegant houses were built to survive and the best of them now serve as inns. In 1663, a merchant built No. 5 to be both a home and business premises and it stayed that way until a Captain Hawkins retired from sailing his boat up the Severn to Wales and opened his inn named after his boat, the Llandoger Trow. Nos. 3 and 4 were added in 1962 when the Bernis took over the inn and made the whole unit into an imposing restaurant on the quayside. The story of the Llandoger has been told many times, but there are one or two other worthwhile inns in this street which are twentieth century con-

The Lightship

FRANK SHIPSIDES - 1979 -

The Nova Scotia

versions of admirable old houses. With Welsh Back at one end and the Frome at the other, it was inevitable that the sea should be very much a part of the scene. The Admiral Benbow and the Naval Volunteer are two recent inns which recall the days of recruiting for the privateer ships which harassed the Dutch and Spanish fleets in the eighteenth century, when sailors who failed to 'volunteer' could be press-ganged into service as they drank their ale in a quayside tavern. The Naval Volunteer is full of ships' fittings and naval relics and it has been opened up internally with skeleton framing which gives a good idea of what a house of the early 1700s was like. John Elbridge, the founder of the B.R.I. once lived in this house.

The Hole in the Wall was originally known as the Coach and Horses, but its more romantic name derives from the interesting little spy-house about four foot square extending beyond the front of the building. As a

Rummer and Parliament Clock, from The Rummer

Llandoger Trow cellar

waterfront inn, it has been the haunt of seafarers for centuries and in the days of the press-gangs it was subject to ruthless raids. Bristol was in fact notorious for its vicious press-gangs and more petitions against their lawlessness emanated from Bristol than from any other city in the kingdom. It is no wonder then that this small room, with the spy-hole on either side, should have become so important. Here, a regular watch was kept and when a look-out spied the predatory gang, sailors in the bars were warned and could make their escape through a long passage at the back to Queen Square.

R. L. Stevenson heads a chapter of his book *Treasure Island*, 'I go to Bristol', and he has young Jim Hawkins meeting Long John Silver at the 'Spyglass' by the dockside. The Hole in the Wall certainly meets the requirements of his description as it stands so conveniently on the Grove opposite Redcliffe Back, with a good view of the waterfront in both directions.

Another inn which has a good view of a different waterfront is the Nova Scotia Hotel, purpose-built in the early nineteenth century to accommodate passengers and horses in the busy Cumberland Basin. The swinging inn-sign shows a full-masted schooner trading in the icy waters of the North Atlantic and this emphasises the inn's links with the sea and ships. The interior of this dockside pub has been little altered over the years and here one can find the true atmosphere of old Hotwells. Regulars come down to the 'Scotia' to drink at a superb mahogany bar with gilded pillars, and the links with ships and sailors are everywhere, in decor, clientele and scenery. Old Bristolians refer to the Scotia as being 'on the island', and Spike Island is the only one in the city docks. Opposite the pub is a row of Dock Cottages, dated 1831, built by the Port Authority for its retired employees. The harbour is full of small craft; a ferry still operates from the slip-way; old salts sit happily on the quayside teaching young fishermen to catch roach, dace and even carp in the Floating Harbour.

Bristol is a city of seamen and shipping and it seems only right that the harbour should be part of its social scene. A positive step has been taken towards opening up the harbour; quays have been landscaped and trees planted; two sites have been set aside for Floating Restaurants within the harbour. The red Lightship, which last saw service off the East Anglia

The White Hart

The Hatchet

~FRANK SHIPSIDES~1978~

The Portcullis, Clifton

40

coast in 1976, is a pub and restaurant, floating in the shadow of Bristol Bridge and within sight of the Llandoger Trow and King Street. The second floating restaurant is the Lochiel, a much larger ship. She retired from serving the Western Isles off the coast of Scotland only to be rescued by Courage (Western) from the breaker's yard and turned into a pub and restaurant in 1978. The forty-year-old Lochiel makes a most attractive restaurant, with all the brass fittings and polished wood of a luxury liner. One can dine in style in the ship's saloon and enjoy a fine view of St. Mary Redcliffe across the water.

Clifton College

More Clifton

UNTIL THE eighteenth century, Clifton consisted of a few houses grouped around St. Andrew's Church and Clifton Green, with a population of at most two hundred. It was really an area of scattered farms, surrounded by heath and woodland, until the development of the Hotwell Spa suggested Clifton Heights as a suitable place to live. Clifton-on-the-Hill soon became an area in which it was fashionbale to live, with its pure air, so different from the smoke-filled city of Bristol.

The first large mansions around the Green were soon followed by long terraces and crescents on the slopes overlooking the gorge and by 1790 speculative building began on a grand scale. Windsor Terrace was the first and most impressive on its magnificent site on the edge of a rocky promontory, but its building led to the bankruptcy of its creator, William Watts. He had amassed a large fortune from his invention of patent lead-shot, but he lost it all on this venture. He had to construct a massive retaining wall and vaults before he could begin the actual houses and a later builder cashed in on Watts' folly as it was called.

Bankruptcy and ruin was the lot of many other businessmen in the 1790s when the French Revolutionary Wars caused Britain's financial collapse and half-built houses stood roofless until the peace came. Royal York Crescent, Saville Place, Bellevue and Cornwallis Crescent, now so

42

-FRANK SHIPSIDES- 1979-

The Paragon

splendid, all spent years in a derelict limbo waiting an injection of capital and courage. Royal York Crescent was the most spectacular scheme and its story one of near disaster. It was planned as the longest, highest and finest Crescent in Europe, a quarter of a mile in length with superb views over to Dundry. Building was begun in 1791 and an immense sum was spent in erecting the deep substructure of vaults and basements required to raise the terrace-walk to a constant level. By 1793 its houses were roofless and fortunes were lost. The builders had left out number 13 calling it 12A instead, but even this did not ward off bad luck. By 1801, the War which had caused its failure almost saw its demise, for when the derelict buildings were offered for sale, the War Office wished to take them over, demolish them and build barracks for the troops whom the local innkeepers had got tired of quartering. Local residents protested that such a building would ruin Clifton as a spa, the scheme was dropped and the Crescent was saved, though the last houses were not finished until 1821. The Crescent was a favourite residence for people of wealth and fashion. Mrs. Thrale was at No. 36, Lord Roberts at No. 25 and the future Empress Eugenie of France spent some of her schooldays at No. 2.

The next expansion took place in the 1840s when the prosperous middle classes wanted their villas in this desirable locality. So, in just over one hundred years, Clifton changed from a small, rural community into the 'village in a city' which it is today. The story of Clifton however, could have had a very different ending, for between the two world wars there was a real danger that it would become a wilderness of 'bed-sitter' land and absentee landlords. The last twenty years have seen a splendid resurrection with the local community restoring houses, cleaning up 'street furniture', revitalising gardens and open spaces, and generally looking after the village so lovingly that once again Clifton is a desirable place in which to live.

The Clifton Village Fayre was first seen in Jubilee Year, 1977, when tradesmen and residents dressed in Regency and Victorian costume ran side-shows, stalls, horse-drawn transport and concerts, in keeping with the atmosphere of that earlier Clifton. The Fayre was an immediate success and has become an annual event coinciding with another attraction, Clifton-in-Bloom fortnight. Clifton has risen, like a phoenix from the ashes, even more beautiful than it was in the past, a splendid example of

Constitution Hill

people accepting their share of responsibility for the place in which they live and work.

One of the nicest aspects of Clifton is its variety: Georgian crescents, Regency terraces, converted mews, the open spaces of the Downs, the Zoo, Brunel's bridge spanning the Gorge. Clifton's parish church, Christ Church has the tallest spire in Bristol. As it stands on the edge of the Downs it is for many the beginning of Clifton proper. It is beautifully sited with grassy slopes on three sides and no churchyard, as it was built in 1840 to be a chapel of ease to St. Andrew's. When that church was 'blitzed', Christ Church was ready to take its place as the parish church for Clifton. The Downs in front of the church look like a pleasant village green, but this was not always so, for the Downs have a history longer than that of Clifton, or indeed of Bristol itself. Just across the green, near the Observatory, the remains of an impressive Iron-age camp may be seen, later used by the Romans as part of their system of fortifications. While the little town of Bricgstowe grew into a city, the Downs remained remote and unfrequented, a natural barrier of heath, furze and woodland, cutting off the villages of Henbury and Westbury. In front of the church, sheep could graze and children skate when the large pond was frozen over, and there were open quarries and lead mines in the near neighbourhood. When the Society of Merchant Venturers purchased the Downs from the Lords of

Christ Church, Clifton

46

the Manor of Henbury in 1861, a great clean-up operation took place. Quarries were filled in, the pond drained, roads laid out, thorn bushes cut down, and the Downs emerged as a recreational and leisure ground for all to enjoy.

The Victorian development of Clifton is best seen in the Promenade, a road of dignified, detached houses of which the most important is the Mansion House. Bristol had been without an official residence for its first citizens since 1831, when the Mansion House in Queen Square was destroyed in the Reform Act Riots. Alderman Proctor was a most generous benefactor and had already given a great deal of money to his city, often anonymously, when he decided to give his new house Elmdale, to be the Mansion House, in 1874. On the first Wednesday in every month, the Lady Mayoress is At Home and between three and five o'clock any Bristolian can just call in, have a cup of tea and see the Civic plate and other treasures. One piece in particular is interesting. This is a sixteenth-century silver salver which was stolen during the Riots, cut into one hundred and sixty-seven pieces by the thief and later sold. The pieces were rescued and riveted together while the thief, James Ives was sentenced to fourteen years transportation. When he had served his sentence, he returned and had the nerve to ask to see the mended salver.

Further along the Promenade, the Society of Merchant Venturers have their new Hall. The Merchants originally met in the disused Chapel of St. Clement granted to them in 1493 by the Corporation, but by 1701 the Society felt the need for a grander Hall to cater for its important role in the city's life. So they erected an imposing building on the same site and they spent a great deal of time and energy beautifying it, paying Thomas Paty £6,000 in 1783 to reface the exterior and remodel the interior. All this went in 1940 when the Prince Street area was badly bombed. The exact site of the Hall is the present Prince Street roundabout, beneath which are the foundations of the medieval Chapel of St. Clement. The Merchants chose a superb house in the Promenade for their new Hall and their Coat of Arms above the door announces their occupation. Some of the treasures connected with the Society were rescued from the damaged old Hall and brought here; the saddle cloth and trappings used by the first Elizabeth on her 1597 visit; the Bristol Cup; a reminder of the days when Race meetings were a popular feature of the Downs; and the W. G. Grace Cup won by him, not for cricket, but for crossing the line first in the West of England Cycling Club's quarter mile race at Bristol Zoo in 1866.

The Victorian middle class demanded more than pretentious mansions in the Promenade, they wanted their sons to be educated in a college whose academic standing would be equal, if not superior to, that of the best public schools. Clifton College was founded in 1862, and by 1877 had received the Royal Charter. The school was lucky in its first Headmaster, Dr. Percival, who had taken firsts in Mathematics, Physics, Classics and History. He got the College off to a good start and its rapid growth in size and numbers was remarkable, growing in fifteen years from sixty to six hundred. Its buildings in honey-coloured stone were developed slowly by C. F. Hansom, whose brother, incidentally, had been responsible for the 'cab' which bears his name. He was committed to the Neo-Gothic style which suited the College's founders, who thought that only such a style could create an environment perfectly suited to the rigorous education of Christian gentlemen. When the College flourished, additional buildings were needed and Hansom supplied these, all in the same style. A small number of tall, gabled houses, in sympathy with the College, were erected nearby in the 1870s, probably to designs by Hansom and when they too became too big for their owners, the College was there to snap them up for boarding houses, so that today the whole area is Clifton College.

Clifton College became a household name in the education world very quickly through the fame of its cricket-field. This is the ground on which W. G. Grace led Gloucestershire to victory in the county championships, and inspired an old boy, Sir Henry Newbolt, to write the well-known lines

> There's a breathless hush in the Close tonight—
> Ten to make and the match to win—
> A bumping pitch and a blinding light,
> An hour to play and the last man in.
> And it's not for the sake of a ribboned coat,
> Or the selfish hope of a season's fame,
> But his captain's hand on his shoulder smote—
> 'Play up! Play up! and play the game'.

Another reputation was made on the playing fields and earned an entry in

48

Clifton Suspension Bridge

Royal Yacht 'Britannia' in the Royal Portbury Dock

the *Guinness Book of Records*. In 1899, 'young Collins' scored the highest number of runs ever recorded in a single innings, when after five afternoons' play, he scored 628, not out. A plaque in the pavilion pays tribute to this old boy and the statue of another old boy, Field Marshal Earl Haig, keeps watch on the Close from the Memorial Arch to old boys and masters who fell in the two World Wars. Other famous old boys include actors Sir Michael Redgrave, Trevor Howard, John Cleese; writers Sir Arthur Quiller-Couch, Roger Fry, T. E. Brown; and explorers Sir Francis and George Younghusband. During the Second World War, the College was used as General Omar Bradley's Headquarters so that it feels entitled to fly the American Stars and Stripes on Independence Day.

―FRANK SHIPSIDES – 1979 ―

The 'Danmark' at Avonmouth

52

The 'Auckland Star' in Royal Edward Dock

Bristol, The Port and The Docks

'BRISTOL IS the sixth largest port in Britain'—so runs the bald statement in the geography book; its connection with the sea and shipping is a more interesting fact. From earliest times Bristol has been a thriving port from which navigators, adventurers and slave-traders have started their voyages to fame and often fortune. As their trade grew so did Bristol and a seemingly never ending campaign for better harbour and dock facilities began. There had been one memorable development in 1247, when it was realised that the eight miles of tidal river which had given Bristol its protection from surprise attack had also limited its development as a port. A remarkable engineering feat was undertaken when the course of the River Frome was changed by digging 'the Great Trench', through St. Augustine's Marsh to join the Avon and the Frome at a lower point. This modestly named Trench changed the shape of the medieval city; an artificial harbour was created, extending from the old place of the bridge as far north as the present Fromesgate House.

Bristol's trade increased locally with Wales and the West for minerals and agriculture; with the continent for wines, fruit and olive oil and most significantly with North America and the West Indies. The next four centuries saw minor improvements to the quays but they also brought argument rather than action, which was to be the keynote of future discussions on the port. The niceties of such esoteric questions as customs dues, wharfage and clannage were the source of endless negotiations between the Corporation and the Society of Merchant Venturers, but the real problem had yet to be faced. The docks were in the heart of the city, at the end of a tidal river whose twice daily ebbing damaged many vessels. When the tide went out, ships keeled over, at least, those that were not in good condition and 'ship-shape and Bristol fashion' did— and many of those so damaged were left to rot and clutter up the harbour.

The first real attempt at improvement began in 1712 when it was decided to construct a dock at Sea Mills, where the Emperor Vespasian had set up his naval transport base in A.D. 43. So, on a creek below the great limestone gorge, not far from the deep water at the Avon's mouth, a private company built the third wet dock in England and sat back hopefully. Its sponsors planned to create a great dockyard saving ships the difficult passage through the gorge, but the hoped for prosperity never came. The dock failed, most probably because, although near Kingroad and attainable at most tides, it was too far from Bristol with which it had no communication except by trow or lighter. The bad condition of the roads also made it just as difficult to haul goods overland. The dock remained a small one, though it is known to have been used by privateers in 1744 and later by whalers. The walls of the lock gates still stand in the harbour but today the only activity is at weekends when small-boat owners give their craft an airing.

The city fathers were once more forced to turn their attention to find some way of improving the docks in the centre of Bristol and overcome the disadvantages of being a tidal harbour. In 1809, William Jessop's scheme was adopted and the New Cut was made diverting the Avon into a new course from Rownham to Totterdown, giving two and a half miles of Floating Harbour to the city and eighty-two acres of new dock accommodation. It is known simply as the Floating Harbour for that is just what it is, a harbour where ships will float no matter what the tide is like, rather than rest dangerously on the river bottom at low tide. The

Seamills

—FRANK SHIPSIDES - 1979 -

Floating Harbour is still a vital part of the city docks and has needed few modifications over the years, but within a few years Bristol found that there was yet another threat to her prosperity, pride and prestige, for the Age of Steam had arrived.

It is indeed ironic that Brunel's prestigious creations the *Great Western* and the *Great Britain* proved to be too large to enter their home port conveniently and moved to her rapidly rising rival, Liverpool. The resultant loss in trade worried the Bristol merchants and an agitation began to find a new deep water site, for only then could Bristol recapture the lost trade and ensure the future. The need however was not so obvious to everyone. Bristol was unique in England in having its docks controlled by a private

The 'Malcolm Miller' at Portishead

-FRANK SHIPSIDES-1979-

56

company and this was detrimental to the port's development. The company charged high dues to increase its profits but the exorbitant costs sent ship-owners to rival ports. A long and bitter battle began. By 1848, the *Bristol Gazette* was forced to remark that 'nothing short of compelling every Dock director to drink a quart of their own fluid, bubbling with the decomposition of animal matter, every two hours, is liable to be effective'. It went on to add that 'at least the company was getting rid of Bristol's surplus population at the same time as it was driving away foreign trade'.

At least fifty schemes for the 'dockising' of the whole river from the city to the mouth of the Avon were put forward by engineers, dock-owners and even one by a minister of religion, but it was obvious that important sections of the community had vested interests in holding up any new dock. Merchants, Corporation and ratepayers just couldn't agree. The real problem was that trade was not increasing sufficiently to improve the old docks and trade could not increase until new docks were built to take the new ships. Caution, hesitation and even double-dealing meant delay, and with each year that passed Liverpool forged ahead.

Ocean-going steam ships were quite unable to face the tortuous route up the Avon, but it was not until 1878 that the truth was finally accepted. Again it was a private company, the Bristol Port and Channel Company, who opened what is still Britain's largest port and the deepest dock in the world, at Avonmouth, proclaiming it open to 'the commerce of the whole world'. Just six years later, the Corporation bought the seven miles of quays and wharves: expansions and improvements quickly followed. The Royal Edward Dock was opened by Edward VII in 1908, complete with granaries, cold-storage and bonded warehouses, grain elevators and oil depots.

A more modest, but none the less useful, expansion took place at Portishead, also in 1878. Taking advantage of a good, natural harbour, a private company built two piers, three landing stages, a lock, a floating and a graving dock. Once again the Corporation bought out the private company.

The success at Avonmouth and Portishead meant the inevitable decline of the city docks. A long political and legal battle over their fate had started as early as 1950, with varying plans for their hypothetical future being put forward. By 1976, a policy decision was taken which kept the docks and their attractive warehouses, but proposed that certain areas of the waterfront be developed with pedestrian walkways, boatyards and marinas, at the same time developing sites for residential, commercial, sporting and cultural uses. The battle is at last over and Bristol has gained. The docks area of the city is coming alive again with sailing, a Harbour Regatta, Rally of Boats and the Grand Prix Power Boat Race and new uses for the redundant warehouses.

Time and tide truly wait for no man and in time even Avonmouth was not big enough to cope with the growing numbers of large cargo vessels using the international routes, Bristol fought yet another battle, this time in parliament and despite political wrangles, reverses and soaring inflation, the Royal Portbury Dock was opened by Her Majesty the Queen in 1977. When the Royal yacht *Britannia* dropped anchor in Royal Portbury the city's future as a major port was once more assured. It well deserves the title Royal, given to it by the Queen herself in her Jubilee Year. It has the largest lock in the kingdom, 140 feet wide, 1,200 feet long, so lengthening the time each day when ships can enter the dock.

Out of centuries of trial, tribulation and turmoil comes triumph and Bristol now has four docks; the old city docks still handle some continental traffic; Portishead caters for the coal, timber and chemical trade; Avonmouth is the terminal for continental and ocean-going cargo ships and Royal Portbury is there ready for the world's container traffic.

Boats at Pill

Entrance to Ashton Court

Ashton Court

In 1960, Bristol Corporation bought the Ashton Court Estate from the last of the Smyth family who had owned the house and grounds for over four hundred years. It was a great bargain. The citizens of Bristol are now free to enjoy all that the one-time exclusive, landowning aristocracy once held; an impressive house, a walled estate, a deer-park and eight hundred and thirty-five acres of woodland. Its new owners in their turn have added further recreational facilities including a nine-hole golf course, nature trail and pony track.

Well, this is how the story of the Smyths of Ashton Court ended, but how did it all begin? The first unassumingly named John Smyth was a successful Bristol merchant, Sheriff and three times Mayor. He had spent a good deal of his time in his Small Street house and business acquiring the wealth necessary to do what all the newly-rich aimed to do, invest in land. In 1545 he bought the Ashton Estate from Sir Thomas Arundell for £920. For that substantial sum he got a fifteenth-century manor house, with a tower, Great Hall, gallery, chapel, kitchens, barns, stables and those eight hundred and thirty-five acres of down and woodland. He continued to lead the life of a busy merchant, but when his grandson Hugh was knighted

Ashton Court Mansion

by James I in 1611, the aristocratic line was established. Hugh's son, Thomas, was elected the M.P. for Bridgwater at the early age of eighteen, and set about keeping up the Mansion in grand style, with thirty-five house servants and the last recorded 'foole' or Jester in private service.

An ardent Royalist, Sir Thomas raised a troop of horse for the King, but he died in 1642 of smallpox, too early to enjoy the glory of the Restoration when his son entertained Charles II at Ashton. Sir Thomas did however begin the extensive building of the south-west wing in an opulent style which befitted his wealth and position. The wing is the most notable architectural feature of the mansion, though incorrectly attributed to Inigo Jones, the Jacobean court architect.

Old houses abound in legends and Ashton Court is no exception. Before leading off his troop of horse to do battle in the Civil War, Sir Thomas gave his steward instructions where to bury the family silver should the Roundheads gain control of the district. Cromwell did besiege Bristol and the faithful steward, not knowing of his master's death, carried out his instructions and buried the treasure. Soon afterwards he also died and the secret was buried with him. Nothing was ever found, but the legend persists that somewhere in those acres lies untold wealth.

The Smyth family was three times afflicted by a lack of male heirs and on the last of these occasions in 1857 Tom Provis, horse thief and forger, walked up to the front of Ashton Court Mansion and demanded that the occupants vacate the premises within two hours in favour of the true heir, himself. He claimed to be the son of the heirless Sir Hugh who had died in 1819. Though he was kicked out unceremoniously by the Smyths, his story was believed by many and he cashed in on his inheritance claims. He set up as a gentleman in St. Vincent's Priory, Clifton, and was accepted as 'Sir Richard'. It cost the Smyths £6,000 to ridicule his claim in court and prove the will to be a forgery. Provis certainly gave them a run for their money, dramatically producing a pig-tail to prove that he was the true heir, as all the Smyth family were supposed to be born with one. For many years this pig-tail was kept under a glass case and shown to callers at the Mansion, but its owner was sentenced to twenty years' transportation for his perjury and pretensions.

By the end of the nineteenth century the Smyths were a major force in the economic and social life of Bristol and North Somerset. As landlords of scores of farms and employers of miners, their wealth and influence was great.

It was under Sir Greville that Ashton Court entered its last and most lavish phase. By 1885 he had spent a private fortune transforming the Mansion into a neo-Gothic fantasy. He rebuilt the central gatehouse with battlemented turrets and a forest of fan-vaulting over the principal entrance. Behind a twelve-foot high, seven-mile long wall, an exotic and exclusive kingdom flourished. The Smyths' private standard fluttered over the gatehouse; rosewalks, fishponds, fountains and statuary abounded in the gardens; three hundred wild deer roamed the downlands, and forcing houses for delicate fruits and trees were tended by an army of estate workers. Sir Greville employed a man to travel all over the world collecting rare birds, butterflies, eggs and nests. He kept a private yacht at Hotwells for cruising in the Mediterranean and when the family went off to Scotland for the shooting season, two trains were needed to transport them and their entourage to the rented Ardross Castle. In 1884 Edward VII came to Ashton Court for Sir Greville's own shooting party when six hundred and three pheasants were 'bagged'. All this cost money, but Sir Greville's Bedminster collieries produced excellent coal for which he received 8½d. a ton in royalties; his miners got 7½d. a ton for digging it out.

By the twentieth century, death duties and a lack of male heirs brought the Smyth empire to an end, though when Sir Greville died in 1901, his widow Dame Emily continued as lady of the manor, opening fêtes and patronising local activities until 1914. She personified the place so much that even today the estate is referred to as 'Lady Smyth's'. Her death cost her daughter, Esmé, a million pounds in duties and the estate never recovered. The fabric of the house deteriorated so much that rain water dripped through the ceilings, but there was still one housemaid employed solely to look after Esmé's twelve Pekinese. It is these dogs who are buried in a corner of the south lawn under a grove of yew trees, each with a name lovingly engraved on a headstone in the Pets' Cemetery.

When Esmé died in 1945, the Smyth family line came to an end. Her nephew could not afford his inheritance and offered the whole estate to Bristol Corporation for £100,000—the exact amount needed to meet the crippling death duties.

The servants' wing, outhouses and winter-gardens have all gone but what remains is magnificent. The Mansion has been partly restored, the Lord Mayor's horses and coach are housed in the stables; the deer park has been restocked and visitors are once more welcome at Ashton Court Estate.

Gamekeeper's Cottages, Ashton Court

Dial House, Westbury-on-Trym

Henbury and Westbury

UNTIL 1935, Henbury could be considered as a Gloucestershire village leading a separate existence from its dominant neighbour four miles away. It was indeed sufficiently important to have been included in an early Charter of Ethelred in A.D. 692 when Bristol itself had no history to record. Henbury, though now part of Bristol, can still be regarded as a huge parish of some 25,000 souls, with a medieval church, a manor house, and the surrounding hamlets of Cribb, Brentry and Coombe within its boundaries. Large modern blocks of flats and modern housing estates have settled down, more or less in harmony, with old buildings and houses from Henbury's earlier days and most fortunately, the old village's roots are visible among this new luxuriant foliage.

It is the Church of St. Mary the Virgin which begins the story, for this was the southern limit of the ancient diocese of Worcester in the Saxon kingdom of Mercia and for centuries boasted a Bishop's palace near the present Blaise House. The palace has gone but the old records survive to tell Henbury's history. We know that there was a church here in Saxon times, but the first reference to the stone building as we know it was in 1093, when Bishop Wulfstan gave it as an endowment to the Benedictine monastery already thriving in the next village of Westbury. Not surprisingly there were frequent quarrels between these near neighbours especially over the rights to tithes, until the Dissolution of the monasteries in 1554 gave both manors to that local snapper-up of church lands, Sir Ralph Sadleir, and left them nothing to quarrel about.

The church itself has of course been altered over the years. The nave still has the base of the massive, late-Norman round pillars from 1175, surmounted by later Early English arches. The Chancel dates from 1270, when Bishop Gifford ordered that his church be beautified. The embellishments continued, but the old fabric needed constant attention and repair culminating in the last great overhaul by G. E. Street, one hundred years ago.

Henbury church is well known to Bristolians for its monuments both inside and out, which are memorials to the most celebrated of the Henbury families who have worshipped there. The most famous, historically and artistically, is the big, black obelisk designed by Thomas Paty to commemorate Sir Robert Southwell. He was Secretary of State for Ireland and it was at his house at Kingsweston that William III stayed in 1690 after his victory at the Battle of the Boyne. Robert's son, Edward, was also Secretary for Ireland and his epitaph in the nave really says it all: 'He enjoyed life with cheerfulness and innocence'. His mother, Elizabeth, had died in 1681 and the church records provide another bit of social history. Her heirs agreed to pay a fine of five pounds so that she could be buried in a linen shroud rather than the woollen one decreed by law which aimed at encouraging England's staple wool trade.

The other monuments are in the churchyard and again two are part of Henbury's history. Near the North door is the fascinating grave of Scipio Africanus, an eighteen-year-old negro slave who died in 1720. His master was the Earl of Suffolk, who lived nearby in the Great House, now demolished. On the headstones, the carved heads of black cherubs grin cheerfully and the inscription reads,

> 'I who was born a Pagan and a Slave,
> Now sleep sweetly a Christian in my grave,
> What tho' my hue was dark, my Saviour's sight
> Shall change this darkness into radiant light.'

This touching verse should perhaps make us revise our ideas about the callousness of the hated eighteenth-century slave-owners, when one was capable of appreciating a valued servant enough to give him a lasting

Henbury Church

monument. The Earl survived his servant by only two months and though there are no memorials to him in the church, this one to his young negro body-servant has ensured the noble Lord's immortality.

Another unusual grave near the vestry door is that of Amelia Edwards, a remarkable Egyptologist. When she died in 1892, an obelisk memorial was erected and on the grave was carved the Egyptian symbol of immortality, a large Ankh, a most unusual sign to find in a Christian churchyard.

The Church Close is a delightful spot on a summer's day, with a small chapel, a war memorial and the Close House spanning the centuries. Close House is a fine, seventeenth century, freestone building with mullioned windows, green copper weather vane and a massive oak door. The top storey was once used as a dormitory for boys at the Charity School opposite, founded by Anthony Edmonds, a Bristol sugar merchant. He left funds in 1624 to be used to build 'some fit houses as a Hospital for the lodging and keeping of Poor boys'. His well-known 'blew boys' survived until 1950, when the foundation was incorporated into the local school system.

The oldest houses in Henbury are the farms, for the village has always been an agricultural community of yeoman farmers, and by the end of the seventeenth century came the first of the opulent country mansions which the Bristol merchants bought with their increasing wealth. The first of these was Henbury Awdelett, now known as the Manor House in the shadow of the church. When John Sampson built it in 1688, it was in the centre of a large park and woodlands, but with the death of the last of the family in 1947, the estate was sold for development. The Manor House, with its gables of Cotswold stone and square porch surmounted by two stone griffins, survived in a small garden and is now used as a Special School for young children.

The next stage in Henbury's greatness came in the eighteenth century when superior dwellings were built on Henbury Hill by all who mattered in Bristol life. Their wealth gave them the desire to become landed gentry and their well-designed houses pay tribute to their taste as well as their social pretensions, and almost all recall a connection with the great of their time. At Vine House lived Dr. Pountny and here in 1775 was born his son, John Decius, who was to become the most famous Bristol Pottery owner of his day. At Henbury House, Richard Champion, the porcelain manufacturer entertained Edmund Burke, that outspoken M.P. for Bristol, who supported American Independence.

The most outstanding estate in Henbury is that of Blaise Castle, bought in 1925 by Bristol Corporation for £20,000, that price to include the Georgian mansion and four hundred acres of parkland and woods. Its story perhaps sums up all the history of large estates in England, an inevitable progression from private estate to public property. When Thomas Farr, yet another Bristol sugar-merchant, wanted to set up as a country gentleman, he chose this beautiful woodland setting for his low-gabled mansion in 1764. He enhanced the view by building a sham Gothic castle on the horizon to serve as a focal point for his woodland walks. This castle is still an interesting Folly in its own right and was kept when Farr's original house was pulled down by the next owner of Blaise, John Scandrett Harford, a Quaker banker. He commissioned the Bristol architect, William Paty, to design his fine mansion which is at the centre of the Blaise Castle Estate. The house was improved by John Nash and by 1810 an Orangery, stables, and a thatched dairy had been added. The mansion is now a Folk Museum housing collections representing life as it would have been lived in the west country since the seventeenth century.

It was the famous landscape gardener, Humphry Repton, who gave the estate its unique character. He began by designing the Gothic gate-house

Looking towards Bristol Bridge

The Goldney Folly

Blaise Hamlet   ~FRANK SHIPSIDES~ 1979~

on Henbury Hill to harmonise with the idea of a Castle and then delighted
in the element of surprise when the visitor found that the castle turned out
to be an elegant mansion. He introduced a timber-lodge, a woodman's
cottage and winding carriage drives to enhance the attractions of the park.
Other attractions have been added for the modern visitor; an old working
corn-mill, a gipsy caravan, and a boating lake all lie in grounds guarded by
the Giant Goram, who—so legend has it—carved out the area and left his
footprint and chair in the rocks for all to see.

So it was that by the end of the eighteenth century, Henbury was well
established as a beauty spot, with coaches bringing regular Sunday trippers
to take their two o'clock 'ordinaries' at the many inns which catered for
this weekly invasion. The Old Crow on the pack-horse road to Wales,

E   69

Sham Castle, Blaise

Thatched dairy, Blaise

The Blaise Inn

Blaise Castle Mansion

70

and the Blaise Inn on another pack-horse route to Gloucester, did a flourishing trade. The present Salutation Inn is a twentieth century anachronism, though there has been an inn of that name on the site for centuries. The name, Salutation, was often given to an inn connected with a church dedicated to St. Mary the Virgin, referring to the angel's salutation to her at the Annunciation.

A visit to Henbury could well end in the peace and seclusion of the picturesque Blaise Hamlet, a group of ten cottages designed by John Nash in 1811 for the pensioners on the Harford estate. The cottages, all different, are grouped around a village green complete with village pump and sundial. They really are so very pretty with thatch, vines and dovecotes in abundance. A Bristol artist, Donald Hughes, bought the whole hamlet in 1943 and generously presented it to the National Trust.

Henbury and Westbury have more than part of their names in common; both were villages of considerable importance before they were incorporated into the city of Bristol. Westbury became a suburb in 1904, but like Henbury it was an established, important ecclesiastical community when Bristol was just a little settlement in the marshes of the Frome and Avon.

Westbury has its river too, though the Trym today is a mere trickle compared to what it was at the beginning of the village's history when it was navigable right up to the church. Viking raiders in fact, sailed up the obliging Trym and destroyed the first Saxon church. Looking at the trickling stream and the pretty village, it takes a tremendous effort of imagination to see it as the scene of rapine and pillage, twelve hundred years ago. The area was too important to be abandoned and when the church was rebuilt as a Benedictine monastery, a new era began for Westbury on Trym. Its prosperity continued and as early as 1286 it was raised to Cathedral status, with a Bishop and fourteen Prebends, including the Reformer Wycliffe, no less, while Bristol had to wait another three hundred years for its cathedral.

Westbury's golden age was undoubtedly the fifteenth century when William Canynges, the builder of St. Mary Redcliffe, became a Dean of the Collegiate Church and its greatest benefactor. He gave the College a new image with, says an annalist, 'a handsome gateway, a high wall, in which he inserted turrets here and there, so that he rendered it more like a citadel than a college'. It was the description, 'more like a citadel' which was to lead to its destruction. In 1643, during the Civil War, Prince Rupert fixed his own Headquarters in the College and before leaving he set fire to the buildings to prevent their occupation by the Roundheads. Part of the 'citadel' still remains in College Road, sympathetically fused into Westminstere Court, a group of purpose-built flats for the elderly.

Westbury is still referred to as 'the village', though its village green, fields and orchards have diminished over the years. Its attraction lies in its small groups of picturesque cottages served by narrow roads, like those at the junction of Channel's Hill and Chock Lane. The old vicarage, painted pink; the Dial House with the hands of the clock fixed at the hour when a former owner was left at the altar; a pack-horse bridge; an old Court House and a Wild-life Park all contribute to the charm of this corner of Westbury on Trym.

Westbury College

-FRANK SHIPSIDES - 1979 -

Westbury Church

73

Stratford Mill, Blaise

~ FRANK SHIPSIDES ~ 1979 ~

William Reeve's Black Castle, Brislington

Some Bristol Follies

ARCHITECTS AND historians agree that no other area has so rich a variety of follies as Bristol. The name folly itself is perhaps unfortunate for the word implies a foolish failure. The men who built the Bristol follies were not foolish, nor were they failures. They were wealthy men who designed follies to add to the beauty of their already attractive estates and each is therefore personal to its creator, often displaying an eccentric charm.

The earliest of the follies and the best known—though least visited— are in the grounds of Goldney House, Clifton. Thomas Goldney the elder, was a Quaker merchant who was one of the first to escape from the smoke of the industrial city and build a new house on the heights of Clifton. It was his son, another Thomas, who developed the garden and the grounds. Goldney House is now a University Hall, but on some summer open days the public can glimpse the life-style of those wealthy merchants and share their enthusiasm for landscaped gardens and the follies which adorn them.

Young Thomas recorded the progress of his schemes in a book which gives details of his intentions and the cost of carrying them out. His first interest was the Grotto and indeed this is still the most unusual and attractive folly in the whole country. He began it in 1737 and records that it took twenty-seven years to complete. The entrance to the Grotto is through a yew hedge from the lawn and into a tunnel with steps leading down to a cavern. The entrance is dramatic enough, but the real surprise comes when one enters the Grotto itself. It is like entering fairyland via one of those transformation scenes which pantomime still delights in. Two realistic stone lions guard the opening of the underground cavern whose walls and pillars are covered with pieces of crystal, minerals, rocks and Bristol 'diamonds'. Thomas Goldney was a shipowner and his captains had instructions to bring home shells and coral from foreign shores to adorn the walls of his Grotto. The result is magical. The roof is of stone carved to simulate water-worn rock and a cascade of water runs into a pool guarded by the marble figure of Neptune.

Many visitors came to see this spectacular creation, including John Wesley and other guests at the Hotwell. Apart from the Grotto, Goldney had other follies to compensate them for the long haul up to Clifton. A Grand Terrace, four hundred feet long was constructed in this town garden from which to take in the view over the river to Dundry on the skyline. At the west side of the Terrace is another folly, a Rotunda built in 1757 as a Gothic summer-house, and enjoying a different view over the river where his ships lay at anchor. A Grand Tower, round and castellated, rises from the Terrace and was the last addition to the garden. It was built to house a 'fire-engine', which provided the steam-power for the cascade of water in the Grotto. The Tower had an internal stairway and there is a further view of Bristol from its battlements. A canal, rosebeds, orangery, and a fine statue of Hercules complete the delights of this twelve-acre garden in the heart of Bristol.

Follies come in all shapes and sizes and one of a very different sort can be found at Brislington, a reminder of the days when Arno's Vale was open countryside and recalling the Arno Valley in Italy after which it was probably named. It was in this quiet spot near the road to Bath, that William Reeve decided to set up his country estate and create his own variety of folly. He first built his house, Mount Pleasant, now Arno's Court Hotel, on one side of the road and opposite two more of his splendid creations. Reeve was a copper-smelter whose occupation provided both the money and the actual material for his first Folly. His house needed stables and other offices to complete it, so he decided to make a virtue out of necessity and erect a perfect 'sham' castle, unique in being a

Arno's Court, Brislington

complete functional building and not just a façade provided to enhance a view. This sham castle is something approaching a true castle in plan; a rectangle of castellated wall enclosing a courtyard with a tall round tower at each corner, and a rectangular keep. The walls of the castle are made of black copper-slag blocks which came from Reeve's Crew's Hole works, and their blackness is dramatically highlighted by the white stone ornamentation. Today it is tucked away behind the main Bath road, but one can imagine the impact it must have made on the eighteenth-century traveller as he approached Bristol through open countryside. Horace Walpole first saw it in 1766 on a visit to Bristol, which incidentally he called 'the dirtiest great shop I ever saw'. He wrote that on approaching

Bristol he 'was struck with a large Gothic building, coal black and striped with white. I took it for the Devil's Cathedral; I found it was a uniform castle, lately built, and serving for stables to a smart, false Gothic House on the other side of the road.'

William Reeve was a great snapper-up of medieval trifles, always on the look-out for anything Bristol didn't want. When St. Werbergh's Church was being taken down some of the monuments disappeared. Felix Farley's *Bristol Journal* was later able to report 'the monumental stone of Nicholas Thorne, founder of the Grammar school, has just been found. It was to have been put up to adorn a gentleman's Gothic stables in the neighbour-hood'. That monument was recovered, but Reeve managed to keep most of his other gleanings. He built a Gateway to his Black Castle in imitation of the old gateways which once stood in Bristol, and when the city demolished those at Lawford's Gate and Newgate, Reeve was there to grab the medieval figures for the canopied niches of his new gateway. Perhaps it is just as well that he did, for the figures are now safe in Bristol Museum. The Gateway still stands, looking forlorn, curiously flattened and out of place on the busy Bath road.

Like all good landscape improvers Reeve continued to embellish his estate. He excavated a tunnel under the road leading to his Black Castle and added a bath house and Moorish colonnade. He was always pleased to show visitors over his follies and enjoyed his reputation as an eccentric. By 1774 he had dissipated all his wealth and bankruptcy ended his career. The house was sold and later altered by its various owners, but the Black Castle has survived virtually unchanged. It has recently been opened as a pub with a liberal sprinkling of instant history: armour, weapons and a minstrel's gallery. The Moorish colonnade and bath house were allowed to deteriorate so much that their demolition seemed inevitable. Sir Clough Williams Ellis rescued them for his fantasy estate in Portmeirion.

The castle which gives Blaise Castle Estate its name is another folly with an interesting history. Thomas Farr, one of those ubiquitous Bristol sugar merchants, paid Robert Mylne £3,000 in 1766 to design a folly which could actually be lived in. He got his castle, a large circular room with four small circular towers around it, castellated and embellished with cruciform arrow-slits. Farr chose a superb site for his folly on a hill top which had once been occupied by early Iron Age camp dwellers as well as by the

The Observatory

later Roman invaders. From its flat roof there are magnificent views of the Avon and Severn valleys and it was this that attracted the visitors. John Wesley didn't spend all his time preaching and Blaise Castle was on his list of follies to be visited, even at the age of eighty. His journal records that he got up at 4 a.m., said his prayers, wrote some letters and then started out from Bristol at 6 a.m. He was enthusiastic about the Castle and wrote that 'Mr. Farr, a person of exquisite taste, built it some years ago on the top of a hill which commands a prospect all four ways as nothing in England excels'. The Castle's original stained-glass windows, plasterwork ceilings and wood staircases have suffered over the years, with vandals adding to the deterioration caused by weather and neglect. A happy solution was found when building apprentices offered to repair it as part of a training scheme, but it will be a long time before the public can again enjoy that famous view from the roof.

Every Bristolian knows the old Observatory which seems to keep a watchful eye on the Clifton Suspension Bridge. It began life as a windmill and was converted into a snuff-mill whose grinding days ended in 1777 when a tremendous gale loosened the sails and the friction set the whole building on fire. It took an artist, William West, to realise its possibilities as a tourist attraction and in 1828 he resurrected it as an Observatory, fitting up the tower with telescopes and a camera obscura. A few years later he excavated a passage to the Giant Ghyston's cave, 335 feet above sea-level, overlooking the Avon Gorge. The Observatory, on the highest point in Bristol, is on the site of an old British camp, whose ramparts can still be traced despite the ravages of time and of the quarrying which took place in this area.

Bristol has lost some of its follies through neglect and even wanton destruction. Cooke's Folly—an ivy-clad tower built in 1696 by John Cooke as an ornament to his country residence overlooking the Gorge—can now only be seen in the many paintings of this area, and is remembered in the name Cooke's Folly Road. Cotham Tower was built about the same time as the Observatory and also started life as a windmill before being turned into a snuff-mill. When the snuff-grinder went bankrupt in 1779, the stone work of the mill was converted into a tower, seventy feet high, to serve as a folly in the grounds of Tower House high on Cotham Hill. When the house was demolished to make way for Cotham Grammar School the tower remained, a splendid landmark on one of Bristol's seven hills. Incredibly, in 1953, it was suddenly and unnecessarily destroyed.

Wickham Bridge

The Frome Valley

IT IS unusual to find even one Nature Trail within a city, but Bristol has many beautiful trails, parkland walks and riverside tracks all laid out for the citizen who wants to take some time off in the country. The most interesting is the Frome Valley Trail.

The Frome rises in Dodington Park and, after pursuing a winding course for some twenty miles, becomes part of the Floating Harbour at the city centre. The most fascinating part of its course is between Stapleton and Frenchay, old villages of considerable charm, and the Frome can be followed for two and a half miles as it flows between these villages. The Frome Valley is an artists' paradise as well as being a profitable hunting ground for amateur geologists, naturalists and industrial archaeologists Quite a bold claim for a short part of a fast-flowing river—the name comes from the Anglo-Saxon 'frume' meaning rapid—but there are some good things between Eastville Park and Frenchay.

Eastville Park is one of the many open spaces in the city preserved as recreation grounds and at all times of the year its ornamental lake abounds in ducks, mallards, moorhens and small boys' boats. The Frome enters

Wickham Glen where, from the fifteenth century onwards, the rapid flow of the river encouraged the building of six mills. Originally these were grist mills for grinding the villagers' corn, but over the centuries underwent many conversions into snuff, iron and flock mills. When steam power replaced water power, mills fell into disuse and their buildings disappeared or fell into ruin, but the weirs still function attractively.

The river has cut a series of small gorges through the pennant sandstone, varying in depth from fifty to eighty feet, and in the Glen they are in marked contrast to the wide, stony beds of its earlier course in Eastville Park. The valley sides have steepened out and outcrops of red pennant rock rise up, so that this miniature gorge takes on the appearance of a many-coloured layer-cake. This part of the river is a favourite haunt of young fishermen hoping to catch tiddlers, gudgeon and pike near Lathbury Mill.

The road to Wickham Bridge is an old Roman route through Stapleton and the bridge is a well-preserved medieval pack-horse passage near the place of an early ferry used by pilgrims to St. Anne's Well. The bridge today is in a quiet backwater but during the Civil War it was the scene of much military activity. A shady lane leads to Wickham Court, a small-sized gabled dwelling, once a farmhouse where history was made. On a hot summer's day in 1645 Roundhead troopers, horses and gun-carriages disturbed the peace of the valley as Cromwell's army rendezvoused with General Fairfax's contingent. A notice over the doorway to Wickham Court records 'Oliver Cromwell and General Fairfax held a Council of War in this house before the attack on Bristol in September 1645. At this Council, Cromwell decided to enter Royalist-held Bristol through Lawford's Gate'. The successful planning at Wickham Court was directly responsible for the defeat of the Cavaliers and brought Charles I one step nearer his death on the scaffold.

Snuff Mills Park is an enchanting spot; seven acres of well laid out gardens with flowering trees, shrubs and plants, and always the fast flowing river with the weirs and abandoned water-wheel of the old mill. One doesn't have to be an industrial archaeologist to appreciate the beauty of this setting and to regret the loss of so much of the original mill.

The other great industry of the Frome Valley was quarrying for red sandstone and the ivy-clad, overgrown rocks of the old quarries are

Wickham Court

reminders of former activity, as are the old quarrymen's cottages which come in groups along the river. Tobacco was grown all along this valley in the last century and was noted as being 'very hot, but cheap'.

The Frome has another surprise in its two-mile course, for after Halfpenny Bridge the valley broadens with a change of soil and vegetation. The scenery is typical of a rocky, damp, tree-lined valley; there are out-crops of rock, ivy-clad slopes, tall trees and fox-earths in the woodlands.

At the end of the valley the river narrows and flows fast over the stones to Frenchay or, as its old name of Fromeshaw implies, 'a small wood by the Frome'. Originally a community of millers and quarrymen, it became a centre in the eighteenth century of a thriving Quaker settlement as wealthy merchants built their handsome houses in superb surroundings. The first large house was Joseph Beck's Manor House which set the pattern for gentlemen's residences on the Common. The architect of this impressive mansion is not known for certain, but it seems likely that John Wood, the elder, had a hand in its design. It is the most opulent mansion in the area but other smaller houses have more interesting connections. It was the Quakers and Unitarians who were responsible for the develop-ment of Frenchay where they hoped to find peace and the freedom to worship in their own way which was denied them within the city limits. Thomas Callowhill came to Frenchay Lodge after marrying Hannah, the daughter of Dennis Hollister who had given the Bristol Quakers their first Meeting House in the Broadmead. His daughter, another Hannah, married William Penn, the founder of Pennsylvania; he must have been a welcome visitor at the house. The Quaker banking family of the Harfords lived at Malmains and Cedar Hall; Joseph Storrs Fry, the Quaker choco-late manufacturer lived at Frenchay Grove, where his cousin, Elizabeth Fry, the prison reformer was a frequent visitor, and to the nearby Friends' Meeting House. The present Meeting House dates from 1809, but there has been a meeting place here since 1673 when the first Quakers dared to hold religious meetings in contravention of the 1664 Conventicle Act which forbade the gathering together of more than five unrelated persons in an act of worship. The punishments meted out were severe and included transportation for the third offence. Sadly, even in this remote hamlet, the law still pursued them and the records are full of the persecutions which this band endured. The secluded garden at the back of the house has

84

Weir at site of Lathbury Mill

-FRANK SHIPSIDES - 1979·

Unitarian Chapel, Frenchay

– FRANK SHIPSIDES – 1979·

been used as a burial ground since the seventeenth century. Quakers were refused burial in any parish churchyard so they were forced to establish their own. At Frenchay it was agreed 'flower borders of eighteen inches wide should be made round the graveyard and sowed with some sort of garden herbs'. Around the edge of the neat garden are flat headstones, all of the same size whether for rich or poor, the names recalling two hundred years of Quaker history.

The Friends' Meeting House marks the beginning of Frenchay Common, a large open space surrounded by elegant houses and the attractive Unitarian Chapel, yet another reminder that the village was an early centre of Non-conformity. Wealthy Unitarians had been able to move out of Bristol as early as 1620 and their chapel has existed in an almost unchanged state since 1691. Built of local pennant sandstone, it has a unique feature, the western bell-tower. The original Unitarians, or Presbyterians as they were once called, welcomed Anglicans to their worship at a time when the nearest parish church was twenty miles away, and they allowed the Anglicans to instal a bell in the tower in 1702. This is the only Dissenting Chapel in the country to have a bell-tower and though a twentieth-century vandal stole the bell for its scrap value, the tower still stands bearing a weather vane depicting Haley's Comet which appeared at the time of the building of the chapel. Behind, in the graveyard, is an immense eight-foot long 'body-snatcher's 'stone. It took eight people to lift this monster slab into position over a newly-dug grave where it was intended to thwart the efforts of local grave-robbers on the lookout for fresh corpses to sell to the eighteenth-century surgeons.

The Common itself is everyone's idea of a typical English country scene with the tall spire of the Parish church visible for miles. Here the great cricketer, W. G. Grace hit out in style as he captained the Frenchay Cricket Club in 1870; in fact all five Graces played here in their time and for over a hundred years cricket matches were a weekend attraction.